G
CE

Novels for Students, Volume 12

Staff

Staff

Editor: Elizabeth Thomason.

Contributing Editors: Reginald Carlton, Anne Marie Hacht, Michael L. LaBlanc, Ira Mark Milne, Jennifer Smith.

Managing Editor, Content: Dwayne D. Hayes.

Managing Editor, Product: David Galens.

Publisher, Literature Product: Mark Scott.

Literature Content Capture: Joyce Nakamura, *Managing Editor*. Sara Constantakis, *Editor*.

Research: Victoria B. Cariappa, *Research Manager*. Cheryl Warnock, *Research Specialist*. Tamara Nott, Tracie A. Richardson, *Research Associates*. Nicodemus Ford, Sarah Genik, Timothy Lehnerer, Ron Morelli, *Research Assistants*.

Permissions: Maria Franklin, *Permissions Manager*.

Jacqueline Jones, Julie Juengling, *Permissions Assistants*.

Manufacturing: Mary Beth Trimper, *Manager, Composition and Electronic Prepress*. Evi Seoud, *Assistant Manager, Composition Purchasing and Electronic Prepress*. Stacy Melson, *Buyer*.

Imaging and Multimedia Content Team: Barbara Yarrow, *Manager*. Randy Bassett, *Imaging Supervisor*. Robert Duncan, Dan Newell, *Imaging Specialists*. Pamela A. Reed, *Imaging Coordinator*. Leitha Etheridge-Sims, Mary Grimes, David G. Oblender, *Image Catalogers*. Robyn V. Young, *Project Manager*. Dean Dauphinais, *Senior Image Editor*. Kelly A. Quin, *Image Editor*.

Product Design Team: Kenn Zorn, *Product Design Manager*. Pamela A. E. Galbreath, *Senior Art Director*. Michael Logusz, *Graphic Artist*.

Copyright Notice

individual does not imply endorsement of the editors or publisher. Errors brought to the attention of the publisher and verified to the satisfaction of the publisher will be corrected in future editions.

This publication is a creative work fully protected by all applicable copyright laws, as well as by misappropriation, trade secret, unfair competition, and other applicable laws. The authors and editors of this work have added value to the underlying factual material herein through one or more of the following: unique and original selection, coordination, expression, arrangement, and classification of the information. All rights to this publication will be vigorously defended.

Copyright © 2001
Gale Group
27500 Drake Rd.
Farmington Hills, MI 48331-3535

ISBN 0-7876-4895-7
ISSN 1094-3552

Printed in the United States of America.
10 9 8 7 6 5 4 3 2 1

Rebecca

Daphne du Maurier 1938

Introduction

"Last night I dreamt I went to Manderley again."
This opening line from *Rebecca* is one of the most
powerful, most recognized, in all of literature. For
more than sixty years, audiences around the world
have praised Daphne du Maurier's novel as a
spellbinding blend of mystery, horror, romance, and
suspense. In this book, readers can see the traditions
of romantic fiction, such as the helpless heroine, the
strong-willed hero, and the ancient, imposing house
that never seems to unlock its secrets. Using
elements familiar to audiences of romances through
the ages, from the moody and wind-swept novels of
the Brontë sisters in the 1840s to the inexpensive

entertainments of today, *Rebecca* stands out as a superb example of melodramatic storytelling. Modern readers considered this book a compelling page-turner, and it is fondly remembered by most who have read it.

The story concerns a woman who marries an English nobleman and returns with him to Manderley, his country estate. There, she finds herself haunted by reminders of his first wife, Rebecca, who died in a boating accident less than a year earlier. In this case, the haunting is psychological, not physical: Rebecca does not appear as a ghost, but her spirit affects nearly everything that takes place at Manderley. The narrator, whose name is never divulged, is left with a growing sense of distrust toward those who loved Rebecca, wondering just how much they resent her for taking Rebecca's place. In the final chapters, the book turns into a detective story, as the principal characters try to reveal or conceal what really happened on the night Rebecca died.

Author Biography

Daphne du Maurier was born in London, on May 13, 1907. Her grandfather was artist and novelist George du Maurier, who drew cartoons for the satiric humor magazine *Punch* and illustrated books, including a few of Henry James' novels; his own novel *Trilby* included a mystic character named Svengali, which has since become a common word in the English language. Her father was Sir Gerald du Maurier, one of the most famous actors on the English stage in the 1910s and 1920s, who first performed the role of Captain Hook in *Peter Pan*. Daphne, along with her sisters, was educated at home. She began publishing short stories in 1928, with the help of her uncle, who was a magazine editor, and her first novel, *The Loving Spirit*, was published in 1931. The following year, she married Major-General Sir Frederick Arthur Montague Browning II. Literary success came quickly. In 1936, she achieved international success with *Jamaica Inn*, a tale of smuggling along the Cornish coast. It was followed in 1938 by *Rebecca*, which became a huge bestseller. Alfred Hitchcock filmed both novels in 1939 and 1940, respectively. Hitchcock also made one of his best-known films, 1963's *The Birds*, from a 1952 du Maurier short story.

For more than twenty-five years, du Maurier lived at Menabilly, a country estate that was the inspiration for Manderley. Her marriage to

Browning was a friendly one but not a loving one, and she kept herself occupied by writing and entertaining friends. The couple's social circle included some of the most famous people of the day, including Sir John Gielgud, Douglas Fairbanks, Jr., and the actress Gertrude Lawrence, who was rumored to have been her lover. Browning's death in 1965 came as a blow to her. She moved from Menabilly to another famous house, Kilmarth, which dated back to the 1300s. The novel *The House on the Rock* is about Kilmarth.

In addition to novels and short stories, du Maurier also published biographies of Branwell Brontë (the brother of Anne, Charlotte, and Emily), of her father and grandfather, and of Sir Francis Bacon. She wrote several plays, including a three-act adaptation of *Rebecca*. Among her autobiographical works is *Myself, When I Was Young* and *The "Rebecca" Notebooks, and Other Memories*. She also wrote several books of local history about Cornwall, where she lived.

Daphne du Maurier died in Par, Cornwall, England, on April 19, 1989, at age of eighty-one. She had not written anything in years, and it was decades since her last important piece of fiction, *The House On the Strand*, was published in 1969.

The Future

The first two chapters of *Rebecca* take place at some undetermined time in the future. The narrator remembers events that happened in the past at Manderley, an English country estate. She and an unidentified male companion are traveling around foreign countries, reminding themselves of the life they once lived by reading the English news in newspapers. This section gives readers a description of Manderley and vaguely mentions other characters that will be important as the story progresses: Mrs. Danvers, Favell, and, of course, Rebecca.

The final paragraphs of the second chapter take the action back in time, to the very start of the story, when the narrator was a companion to Mrs. Van Hopper and was staying at the hotel Cote d'Azur at Monte Carlo.

The Hotel Cote d'Azur

Mrs. Van Hopper is presented as a greedy, vain, patronizing woman who likes to think of herself as entering European high society, although she clearly is too ill-mannered to do so. Her companion is a poor young woman who could never afford to be in such an expensive resort by herself.

When Mrs. Van Hopper sees Maxim de Winter, she recognizes him and asks to sit at his table, using the excuse that he and her nephew know each other. She does not recognize his impatience with her, although the narrator does. Later, after they have gone back to their room, de Winter sends a note to the narrator, apologizing if he has been rude.

The next morning, Mrs. Van Hopper becomes ill, and her companion finds herself with free time. She has lunch with de Winter, and then they start meeting regularly for rides in the country in his car. She tells him about her life, but he hardly talks about his. From Mrs. Van Hopper's gossip, she knows that his wife died in a boating accident about eight months earlier, and that he owns the estate known as Manderley.

When Mrs. Van Hopper decides that she wants to return to America, the narrator tells de Winter. He returns to Mrs. Van Hopper's room with her and explains that her companion will not be going with her, that they are in love and going to be married.

The Uncomfortable Months

After a few weeks of honeymooning in Italy, Maxim de Winter returns to Manderley with his wife. Not having come from a wealthy background, she is intimidated by the responsibilities of being the mistress of a huge estate. She is uncomfortable with giving orders to the servants. They respond to her discomfort in different ways. Frith, the senior butler, is patient with her uncertainty and is willing to offer polite suggestions as to ways that she might want to handle things, if she wishes, always making it clear that domestic situations are hers to command. On the other hand, there is Mrs. Danvers, who came to Manderley when de Winter was first married to his first wife, Rebecca. Mrs. Danvers does not allow anything to be changed in Rebecca's bedroom, keeping it exactly as it had been when she was alive. She also corrects the new Mrs. de Winter when she tries to change the way that Rebecca did things. Maxim is hesitant to talk about Rebecca, and so the narrator assumes that he is tortured by the memory of their love.

Once, while walking out near the shore, her dog (who had been Rebecca's dog) leads her to a cottage that is falling apart in disrepair. There, she meets Ben, a retarded young man who talks in mysterious half-sentences, frightening her. When she tells Maxim that she met Ben in the cottage, he is upset to hear that the cottage was unlocked, making her suspect that he wants it to remain unchanged, the way Rebecca left it.

One afternoon, while Maxim and the other servants are away, she finds Mrs. Danvers with a strange man, who introduces himself as Jack Favell. He is loud and aggressive, although he asks her not to tell Maxim that he was in the house. Later, from Maxim's sister, she finds out that Favell was Rebecca's cousin. Maxim finds out that Favell was there and reprimands Mrs. Danvers, who, walking away, gives Mrs. de Winter a scornful, piercing stare.

The Masquerade

After local people keep asking Mr. and Mrs. de Winter if they are going to have the grand costume ball, which has been a long-standing tradition at Manderley, Maxim agrees to go ahead with it. Mrs. Danvers suggests to Mrs. de Winter that she might want to have her costume patterned after one of Maxim's ancestors, pictured in an oil portrait in the hall. She agrees and draws a sketch of the picture of Caroline de Winter, which she sends to a costume maker in London that Mrs. Danvers has recommended. She waits with growing excitement for the day of the ball, certain that it will be her chance to show off as the mistress of the house.

Before the party begins, she walks downstairs in her costume, only to find Maxim and her close friends horrified: the costume is the same one that Rebecca wore to the last ball at Manderley. Maxim, in a rage, shouts at her to go upstairs and change. She thinks about staying in her room all night, but Maxim's sister Beatrice convinces her to attend the ball in a regular dress and explain to the guests that the costume makers had sent the wrong package. Throughout the whole evening, Maxim stays away from her, and when he does not come to bed that night, she becomes convinced that he hates her for desecrating the memory of Rebecca.

The Sunken Boat

The next day, while she and Mrs. Danvers are arguing, word comes that a ship has run aground in the bay. The divers who are sent to assess the damage find a greater surprise: at the bottom of the sea is Rebecca's boat, with a dead body in it. That night, Maxim explains to his wife that he lied when he identified Rebecca's body, miles upshore, months after her disappearance. The body in the boat is hers. He put it there after he killed her, and then he sank the boat. He was not, after all, living with grief over Rebecca because she was a cruel, spiteful, promiscuous woman. His love for his new wife is true.

When the body is identified as Rebecca's, there is an inquest. Just before the case is closed, with the finding that she became trapped in the boat when it sank, it is revealed that the boat would not have sunk on its own, that someone pounded holes into it from the inside. Mrs. de Winter, fearing Maxim's exposure, leaves the courtroom in a faint, but she later finds out that the verdict was that Rebecca committed suicide.

Favell shows up that night with a letter that Rebecca sent him on the day she died, asking him to meet her that night; he says that it proves that she did not plan suicide. When Maxim refuses to pay blackmail, the local magistrate is called. He does not believe Favell's claim that he and Rebecca were lovers, and when Ben is called in to testify about seeing them together, he refuses to say anything, afraid that they mean to commit him. The next day they all drive to London to see the doctor that Rebecca had consulted. He tells them that she had cancer and was going to die a painful death. The magistrate accepts this as evidence of her suicide, and on the drive home, Maxim guesses to his wife that Rebecca goaded him into killing her.

The narrator explains that they later found out that Mrs. Danvers received a long-distance call, probably from Favell, and that she packed her belongings and left Manderley in a hurry. The last paragraph of the book describes the closing scene in which, returning from London, Mr. and Mrs. de Winter come around a corner to find the house engulfed in flames.

Characters

Ben

Ben is a mentally retarded man who lives near Manderley and spends his time near the cove where Rebecca kept her boat. When he first shows up, speaking in riddles that she does not understand, he frightens Mrs. de Winter. When Favell is trying to prove that he and Rebecca were lovers, he sends for Ben as a witness that he was a frequent night visitor to the cottage where she often slept. Ben is confused, however, and afraid that the authorities have sent for him to put him in an asylum, and he refuses to say anything about what he knows.

Media Adaptations

- In 1977, as part of the celebration of

her seventieth birthday, Daphne du Maurier participated in a television biography about her life. This rare interview by Cliff Michelmore, entitled *The Make Believe World of Daphne du Maurier*, is available in VHS cassette from Banner Films in London.

- *Rebecca* is one of director Alfred Hitchcock's most celebrated films, made in 1940 with Laurence Olivier and Joan Fontaine.

- *Rebecca* was also adapted to a television series on the British Broadcasting System in 1978 starring Jeremy Brett, Joanna David, and Anna Massey, with direction by Simon Langson.

- A 1996 adaptation of the book, co-produced by Carlton-UK television and WGBH-TV in Boston, stars Charles Dance, Diana Rigg, and Faye Dunaway. This version is directed by Jim O'Brien with a screenplay by Arthur Hopcraft.

- A 1993 abridged audiocassette version of the book, read by Jean Marsh, is available from Audio Renaissance.

- There is an unabridged audiocassette version, released in 1999 by Audio

Partners Publishing Company, which is read by Anna Massey, who played Mrs. Danvers in the 1978 British television version.

Frank Crawley

Frank is the manager of business affairs at Manderley, an efficient and faithful employee who, though boring, is always extremely tactful about what he says in social situations. Soon after she meets him, Mrs. de Winter feels that she can trust Frank. When she is uncomfortable about how Maxim might feel about his dead wife, Frank assures her that she is just what Maxim needs, making him one of her first friends at Manderley. She even feels comfortable enough with him to ask him directly if Rebecca was beautiful, and he replies: "I suppose she was the most beautiful creature I ever saw in my life." From this she assumes that he, like everyone else, was in love with Rebecca. Later, when Maxim tells her the truth about Rebecca, he explains that Frank had wanted to quit his job because she kept pestering him sexually and would not leave him alone. When Maxim is accused of killing her, it becomes clear that Frank knows he really is guilty and probably knew all along, although he has remained quiet.

Mrs. Danvers

Mrs. Danvers came to Manderley as Rebecca's maid soon after Rebecca and Maxim were married. She is very formal and intimidating toward the new Mrs. de Winter, showing her how things are done at the house and practically insisting that the traditions that Rebecca started be continued. She has two encounters with Mrs. de Winter that are particularly odd. In the first, Mrs. de Winter goes for the first time to the rooms that Rebecca occupied after seeing Mrs. Danvers in the window with a strange man, who turns out to be Jack Favell. While she is in the room, Mrs. Danvers comes in and, as if she is a curator in a museum showing off a prized collection, shows her Rebecca's belongings. She touches the bed, the clothes, and the hair brushes adoringly. She says that she allows no one else into Rebecca's rooms, that by keeping them intact it is like Rebecca has never really left, remarking that "It's not only in this room…. It's in many rooms in the house. In the morning-room, in the hall, even in the little flower-room. I feel her everywhere. You do too, don't you?"

It is Mrs. Danvers who suggests the costume for the ball that makes Maxim angry with his wife because it is the same one that Rebecca wore. The evening of the ball, she sees Mrs. Danvers in the hall, an evil smile on her face: "The face of an exulting devil."

On the day after her humiliation at the masquerade ball, Mrs. de Winter finds Mrs. Danvers in Rebecca's room. Mrs. Danvers tells her directly that she should never have come to

Manderley, and, recognizing her misery, stands beside her at the window, urging Mrs. de Winter to jump and kill herself before they are interrupted.

Later, it becomes clear to Mrs. de Winter that it was Mrs. Danvers, with the help of Favell, who set Manderley afire before disappearing.

Maxim de Winter

When he first appears at Monte Carlo at the beginning of the novel, Maxim is the mysterious, handsome forty-two-year-old stranger who has suffered the tragic loss of his wife eight months earlier. After a brief courtship, he asks the book's narrator to marry him, and he takes her back to his country estate, Manderley, which is famous all over the world. Whenever his late wife, Rebecca, is mentioned, he becomes excessively emotional. He and his new wife move into a wing of the house on the far side of the one he occupied with Rebecca. He encourages her not to do things that Rebecca did. She assumes this to mean that he still mourns the memory of his late wife and is not willing to let Rebecca's place in his heart be taken by another.

Once the boat that Rebecca died in is found, Maxim confesses the truth to his wife: Rebecca was, in spite of the glowing praise of almost everyone who knew her, a spiteful, bitter woman who threatened to make him responsible for her child by another man, and in a fit of rage he killed her. The most incriminating piece of evidence against him is that he identified a body that washed up on the shore far away, months after her disappearance, as Rebecca. Because he is well liked in the community, the officials are willing to accept that his identification was a mistake. There is no evidence of foul play on the corpse that they find on the sunken boat because Maxim's shot passed through her heart without touching any bone.

For several of the book's final chapters, Rebecca's cousin, Jack Favell, questions Maxim's innocence, first trying to blackmail him and then, when Maxim calls his bluff, insisting that the authorities investigate further. Maxim does not lose his composure by denying Favell's accusations or trying to prove them wrong; instead, he risks exposure by agreeing to any steps that might prove him guilty. In the end, when it is found out that Rebecca was not pregnant but that she was, in fact, dying of cancer, he guesses that she actually wanted him to kill her, that she wanted to die without suffering and to leave him with the guilt of her murder.

Mrs. de Winter

The narrator of this book is never called by her given name. Not until she is married to Maxim de Winter is she directly referred to by name. She was a poor orphan, whose parents both died within five weeks of each other. She took a job as companion to the wealthy American, Mrs. Van Hopper, with whom she is staying at Monte Carlo in the south of France when they meet Maxim de Winter.

After Maxim marries her and takes her back to his estate, Manderley, she feels self-conscious about her position as mistress of the house. In her embarrassment, she leaves the details of the house to the servants, thus permitting them to continue with the patterns they had become used to under Maxim's late wife, Rebecca. She allows herself to be bullied by Rebecca's personal maid, Mrs. Danvers, who continually corrects her about how things should be done, remarking that "Mrs. de Winter," meaning Rebecca, arranged things. Mrs. Danvers is always ready to embarrass the new Mrs. de Winter by pointing out her timidity; however, the other servants and laborers at Manderley, as well as people who live nearby and stop there, are kind to her.

When Maxim agrees to throw a grand costume ball at Manderley, his wife, at the suggestion of Mrs. Danvers, orders a costume that reproduces the gown and wig worn by a de Winter ancestor in one of the mansion's oil paintings. As the party approaches, her childish excitement rises to a fevered pitch, but when Maxim sees her costume, he loses his temper and tells her to take it off—it is identical to the one Rebecca wore at the last ball before her death. She hides in her room, but eventually comes out in an ordinary dress from her closet and performs her duties as a hostess although she feels that she has insulted Maxim and has been humiliated by him.

It is the day after the ball that the boat in which Rebecca died is found. A series of events, which include accusations of murder aimed at Maxim and a formal inquest, follows. Throughout the rest of the book, the narrator relates the action and describes her concern, but her involvement is minimal.

Jack Favell

When the narrator first encounters Favell, he has been sneaked into Manderley by Mrs. Danvers. He is there on a day when the other servants are off, and his car is hidden behind the house. He is a bold, annoying man, who makes leering, suggestive remarks, offering Mrs. de Winter cigarettes and asking her to go for a ride in his car. He is obviously familiar with the estate: the young dog, Jasper, knows him, and he refers to Mrs. Danvers as "old Danny." She later finds out that he is Rebecca's cousin and that Maxim does not want him in the house. In addition, he and Rebecca were lovers; Favell contends that at the time of her death, Rebecca was planning to run away with him and marry him.

Favell is the driving force for the action in the book's later chapters. Upset that an inquest has determined that Rebecca died by suicide, he shows up at Manderley with a note that she sent him on the afternoon of the day she died, asking him to meet her that night as she had something important to tell him. Using this as proof that she did not intend to kill herself, he attempts to blackmail Maxim, and when that does not work, he insists that the authorities be called to investigate, leading them to call Ben as a witness, to go through Rebecca's diary, and, finally, to drive to London to interview her doctor. At last, Favell gives up. Outside of the doctor's house, he is feeling sick. Maxim and his wife find out later that Favell actually returned to Manderley to take Mrs. Danvers away, starting the house on fire before they left.

Frith

Frith has been a servant at Manderley since Maxim was a child. He is faithful, performing his duties without ever letting any opinions or suspicions be known.

Colonel Julyan

The Colonel is the magistrate of Kerrith, the leading law official in the county. He is a guest at the masquerade ball, and, two days later, he dines at Manderley after Rebecca's sunken boat has been raised and her skeleton found. In spite of the tension in the room, the Colonel makes small talk with Mrs. de Winter until the servants have left the room, and it is only then that he is open about the sunken boat.

When Favell makes accusations against Maxim, Colonel Julyan is brought in to investigate. At first, he is obviously disgusted by Favell's drunken state, but he weighs the evidence carefully. His eventual determination is that there is plenty of evidence for believing that Rebecca committed suicide and little reason to think that she did not.

Maxim de Winter, however, believes in the end that the Colonel can tell he is guilty but content to let the matter be forgotten.

Beatrice Lacy

Maxim's sister, Beatrice, is the opposite of his wife. She is tall, athletic, and outspoken. At first, she seems intimidating, and the narrator does not think that they will get along. Still, Beatrice (or "Bee," as her friends call her) is fond of the narrator. Her wedding present to the couple, a set of books about the history of art, is chosen because one of the few things she knows about her new sister-in-law is her interest in drawing. She takes Maxim's wife along with her when she goes to see their grandmother, to introduce her to the only other member of Maxim's family.

When Mrs. de Winter mistakenly upsets Maxim by wearing the same costume to the Manderley ball that Rebecca once wore, Beatrice helps her get over her humiliation, picking out an ordinary dress from her closet and telling her that it will look fine on her. Although her assertiveness in social affairs is useful in that case, it becomes dangerous later. After a coroner's inquest finds that Rebecca committed suicide, Beatrice, not knowing that Maxim killed her, tells her sister-in-law to insist that they open the case again because she thinks that a suicide verdict is a humiliation to her brother. At the time, her son is home from school with the measles, and no one is allowed to leave the house, so she is not able to raise a fuss that could have exposed her brother's guilt in the crime of Rebecca's murder.

Major Giles Lacy

Beatrice's husband is something of a stereotype: a big, dull, jovial man, who recedes into the social background behind his brash, domineering wife. When Maxim discloses the truth about Rebecca, he mentions that it was obvious from Giles' loud, boisterous manner when he and Rebecca came back from an afternoon of boating that they had had a fling.

Robert

Robert is the assistant butler at Manderley. He performs the duties, such as going to the post office, that Frith is incapable of doing.

James Tabb

Tabb is the shipbuilder who performed yearly maintenance on Rebecca's boat. After it is pulled from the harbor, people said that he had not maintained it properly, and Tabb, to save his professional reputation, inspected it. He testifies at the inquest that the boat sank because of holes deliberately put in it from the inside, a fact that nearly causes great trouble for Maxim before the coroner declares it an act of suicide.

Mrs. Van Hopper

At the beginning of the book, the narrator is employed as a companion to Mrs. Van Hopper, a rich and pretentious American woman. She is a social climber, trying to ease into upper-class European society by introducing herself to its finest members. In the case of Maxim de Winter, she uses snapshots that some mutual friends have sent her from their vacation as an excuse to sit at his table and have lunch with him. After de Winter tells her that he is in love with her companion and is taking her away to marry her, Mrs. Van Hopper offers her congratulations, but when he leaves, she raises doubts in the narrator's mind:

> "Of course," she said, "you know why he's marrying you, don't you? You haven't flattered yourself he's in love with you? The fact is that empty house got on his nerves to such an extent he merely went off his head. He admitted as much before you came into the room. He just can't go on living there alone …"

Themes

Loyalty

The driving force behind the actions of this book's characters is loyalty. This is seen most clearly in the characters of Frank Crawley, the business manager of Manderley, and Frith, the head butler. Crawley expresses his loyalty by being congenial, never shying away from a topic of conversation and yet never expressing exactly what he thinks either. Mrs. de Winter can sense that Crawley is on her side, but she also knows that he will not be completely honest about what he thinks of Rebecca because his sense of loyalty to Maxim would forbid it. Frith is just as deeply loyal, but it is easier for him to keep up his attitude of detachment because, as a servant, he is not involved in family matters nor expected to know about the de Winters' affairs anyway.

Like Frith, Mrs. Danvers is a family servant, but her sense of loyalty makes her negligent in her duty. She is loyal to Rebecca, the dead member of the family, and, in her attempt to preserve Rebecca's memory, she is disrespectful to the current Mrs. de Winter. At first, her loyalty appears as just an annoying, but almost respectable, personality tic, as when she tells the narrator that certain practices are followed because "that is the way Mrs. de Winter wants it done," ignoring the fact that the person she is talking to is now Mrs. de Winter. After the costume ball, her hostility becomes open, and she tries to capitalize on the narrator's grief at her inability to fit in by urging her toward suicide, because "You tried to take Mrs. de Winter's place." In the end, her loyalty to Rebecca's memory makes it impossible for Mrs. Danvers to accept that the new Mrs. de Winter and Maxim can be happy together, so she burns Manderley down.

The narrator's greatest concern, however, is her suspicion that, despite having married her, Maxim is loyal to the memory of Rebecca. She reads his moodiness to mean that he is still grieving over his lost wife. His refusal to use the bedroom that he used with Rebecca, his refusal to go near the cottage Rebecca used, and his anger at seeing her wear the same costume Rebecca wore all seem like signs that he is not willing to give up the memory of her. In the end, when he admits to having actually hated Rebecca and killed her, the narrator does not even think of leaving him because he is a murderer; she stays loyal to him throughout the investigation because she loves him.

Flesh versus Spirit

Part of the narrator's sense of inferiority results from the fact that she is competing with the memory of a dead woman. Her sense of what Rebecca was like builds up slowly from isolated clues: the inscription in a book, her formal agenda left in her desk, Mrs. Danvers' description, and the descriptions of all of the people who knew her. The most uncomfortable comparison comes from Maxim's grandmother who, at eighty-three, is senile and unpredictable: in the middle of their conversation, she loses touch with reality and calls out, "I want Rebecca, what have you done with Rebecca?" There are several practical reasons that the narrator feels she cannot compete with Rebecca, as she finds out about her beauty and social grace. She also is unable to compete because Rebecca is just a memory and therefore is incapable of doing wrong, while she, being human, is quite fallible. Rebecca's continuing presence in Manderley is manifest in the way she decorated it, in her schedules and customs (such as the daily approval of the menu), and in the words of praise visitors have for her. She haunts the narrator as much as if she actually occupied the house like a ghost. "Sometimes I wonder," Mrs. Danvers tells her, as they are looking at Rebecca's belongings. "Sometimes I wonder if she comes back here to Manderley and watches you and Mr. de Winter together."

The ironic thing is that the ghost of Rebecca that haunts Manderley is more a result of terror than of grief. Maxim de Winter remembers her as a mean-spirited woman who put on a sickly sweet image before the public. If he is haunted by her, it is because of his own internal struggle with the guilt he feels for killing her, not because he misses her at all. Frank Crawley's elusiveness about Rebecca, which the narrator thinks is because of his suppressed love for her, is actually discomfort, because she put him in an awkward position by making sexual advances toward him. Beatrice and Giles cannot speak of her memory clearly because they both know that she seduced Giles, and so, unsure of how to speak of her, they end up talking about her with polite praise. In the formal British setting of this novel, people find it better to speak well of the dead than of the living.

Topics for Further Study

- Monte Carlo is still recognized around the world as a vacation spot for the rich. Research what it was like in the 1930s: what sort of people went there, what sort of activities were available, and so forth.

- Using the descriptions in the novel, draw sketches of various locations at Manderley.

- Write a short story about where Maxim de Winter and his wife will eventually end up after they finish traveling, as described in the very first chapters. Bear in mind that this novel ends at just about the time that World War II begins.

- The novel describes how Rebecca threatened to have someone else's child and make Maxim de Winter raise it as his own. Research British law and try to find out how difficult it would have been, in the 1930s, for him to divorce her.

- Several times in the novel, the characters predict what the weather will be like, with observations such as "the glass is dropping." Explain how a barometer works and how accurate its predictions are likely to be.

- *Rebecca* is still popular today. Find out the sales figures throughout the years. Try to explain at least one period of high or low sales.

Guilt and Innocence

One of Daphne du Maurier's greatest achievements in this novel is to convince readers of the innocence of the murderer and the guilt of the murder victim. There are several reasons why, according to the novel's moral structure, Rebecca deserved to die. For one thing, she was cruel and a liar: as Maxim explains it, "They all believed in her down here, they all admired her, they never knew how she laughed at them behind their backs, jeered at them, mimicked them." Mrs. Danvers repeats Rebecca's falseness when she bursts Favell's delusion that she loved him: "Love-making was a game with her, only a game. She told me so. She did it because it made her laugh." Another reason Rebecca deserved her fate is the fact that she was promiscuous: when the truth comes out about her, the list of men she was with or tried to seduce includes Favell, Crawley, Giles, and, presumably, a lot of others, first in London, and then, increasingly, at her cottage at Manderley, where she would invite men for "picnics." In addition, there are perversities that are not described in the book, things that she told to Maxim that he says, with a shudder, "I shall never repeat to another soul." The ultimate offense, the one that drives him to shooting her, is that she threatens to have another man's child and tell everyone that it is Maxim's so that the child would be raised bearing his name: "And when you died Manderley would be his. You could not prevent it. The property's entailed."

Maxim's innocence in killing Rebecca stems from the fact that it is a selfless act: he is not protecting himself, but the good name of Manderley, which her exploits threaten to destroy. To the narrator, Maxim's pureness of heart, his love for her, and his devotion to Manderley are more important than the fact of the murder he committed. They find out in the end that Maxim was even less guilty than they had assumed him to be because Rebecca had cancer and was going to die anyway. One last factor in mitigating Maxim's responsibility for what he did is his guess that Rebecca goaded him into shooting her, so that she could die a quick and painless death and make him feel guilty about doing what cancer would have done in a few months anyway. Readers are left with the impression that Rebecca is guilty and that Maxim, who actually killed her and buried her at sea, is a victim of circumstances.

Setting

There are two main settings for this novel. The first is the resort of Monte Carlo on the southern coast of France. Since 1862, when the first gambling casino was opened there, the town has been famous around the world as a playground for Europe's rich. Starting the book in this setting serves to establish the wealthy social class of these characters. It also helps to raise readers' curiosity about Manderley, which is talked about constantly, even by characters who have never been there but who know it by reputation. The narrator buys a postcard of Manderley in a shop in Monte Carlo.

Most of the book tales place at Manderley, the English country estate that has been owned by the de Winter family for generations. The house itself is imposing to a young girl who was not raised in this wealthy social environment. It is so large that she gets lost, so large that one entire wing can be shut off with Rebecca's personal belongings with little effect. Ancient portraits hang on the walls, reminding the narrator of the responsibility of becoming part of a well-established dynasty. The place is decorated with expensive things that Rebecca put there, constantly reminding her of the presence of the first Mrs. de Winter.

The house is surrounded by trees, which can be

inviting on a sunny day but frightening on a dark, rainy one. Past the trees is the bay. Manderley's proximity to the sea is important because it adds to the beauty of this rich estate but also because the sea hides the corpse of the murder victim, but hides it in a way that it can be found again. One other significant aspect of Manderley is the mysterious cottage where the narrator encounters Ben: this place is left to decay, obviously because Maxim cannot bring himself to go there, raising the prospect of mystery until the end, when it turns out to be central to the horrible events of the past.

Structure

Most of *Rebecca* follows a chronological path, from the time the narrator meets Maxim de Winter at Monte Carlo to the night that Manderley burns down. There is, however, a prelude that takes place some time after the events in the novel. There is no way to tell when this beginning section, which comprises the first chapter and a half, takes place, only that the events that happened at Manderley still haunt the narrator and her male companion, who is left unidentified.

The function of this beginning is to foreshadow events that the reader is going to read about. Mrs. Danvers is mentioned, and so are Jasper the dog and Favell. They are all brought up in the natural way that they might pass through the mind of someone thinking about the past. Because readers do not know what these names refer to, however, they serve in these first chapters to focus attention, to keep readers alert for the story that is about to unfold. The most important element of this introduction is the fact that the man travelling with the narrator is not identified: while reading the main story, readers have to be alert to signs that her love affair with Maxim de Winter might end and to look for clues that hint who her true love might turn out to be.

Gothicism

The true flowering of the gothic novel was during the late eighteenth and early nineteenth centuries when it was a sub-category of the much broader romantic movement in literature. While romanticism explained humanity's relationship with nature as one of mutual benefit, with nature providing an escape from the rules of society and offering artistic souls a chance to express themselves creatively, Gothicism stressed the frightening, dark, unsure aspects of nature. The most powerful example of the gothic novel is Mary Wollstonecraft Shelley's *Frankenstein*, which is concerned with the tragic results that can occur when humans tamper with nature.

Gothic novels usually include elements of the supernatural, mystery, and horror. In *Rebecca*, all of the events end up being explained within the realm of commonly understood reality, but the haunting "presence" of Rebecca's personality gives the book a Gothic mood. Another key element of these works is their setting in ancient castles, usually decaying, which is an element that shows the romantic movement's fascination with ancient history along with the Gothic interest in death and decay. The short stories of Edgar Allan Poe contain many of the most recognizable Gothic elements. Many of the novels that modern readers associate with romance and horror use elements of Gothicism.

Narrator

Readers are often so comfortable with the narrative voice used in this novel that they can finish the entire book without realizing how little they know about the woman who is telling the story. Du Maurier does not even provide a name for this person. She is described as being small and girlish, with a pageboy haircut. (Frank Crawley suggests that she might be Joan of Arc at the masquerade because of her hair.) The book does not, however, tell how old she is nor where she was raised nor how she came to work for Mrs. Van Hopper, her employer when the story begins. She does like to draw, but not so much that she practices her interest within the story, and she seems perplexed by the books on art history that Beatrice gives her. It is not until the seventh chapter that any of the other characters addresses her directly, and then it is as "Mrs. de Winter," a title that identifies her in relation to her husband.

Du Maurier manages to keep her readers from being curious by having this narrator describe the things around her with such fascination and loving detail that all attention is drawn to them. The people and events that she encounters fill her imagination, and she in turn fills the reader's imaginations with her descriptions. Maxim de Winter, in particular, is so important to her that she focuses her story on him. Furthermore, this narrator has such a complete, believable personality, which comes out through her telling of the story, that readers find that they are not curious about her past.

Post World War I

During the 1800s, Britain had built its empire by adding colonies, dominions, and protectorates. These were the great years of the British Empire: Queen Victoria, reigning for over sixty years, gave the nation a sense of stability and progress. Her conservative social views created the stiff-lipped, formal stereotype of the British citizen that is known today and that is portrayed in *Rebecca:* strict rules of behavior between the sexes, tea at four-thirty each day, and a fascination with wealth that was suppressed by the good taste not to talk about it. When Victoria died in 1901, her son Edward succeeded her to the throne. The Edwardian age in England is considered a time of international stability, owing to Edward VII's talent for negotiations. Like the Victorian era, Edward's reign from 1901 to 1910 was marked by domestic stability and social formality.

World War I shattered the tranquility of Europe, especially of Great Britain. Previous military conflicts, such as the Crimean War and the Boer War, had been marked by the civility of the participants. In the previous battles, the British class system had been clearly maintained, separating officers from soldiers, keeping the former far from the fighting, in deference to their ranks. World War

I, on the other hand, brought new technology that destroyed any sense of class in battle. Long-range cannon, portable machine guns, and, especially, the use of poisonous gas forced the genteel tradition to wake up to the inhumane horrors of modern warfare.

Being with the winning forces, Britain benefited at the end of the war; colonies that had been under German control became British mandates. For a short while, there was a postwar economic boom as laborers returned and industry grew. The old social class system, though, with the type of rigid structure that du Maurier presents in *Rebecca*, was on its last legs as modern technology made the feudal system that great estates like Manderley were built upon seem increasingly pointless.

Compare & Contrast

- **1938:** The first nuclear fission of uranium is achieved by German scientists. This is the physical reaction that leads to the nuclear bomb.

  1945: Nuclear bombs are dropped on the Japanese cities Hiroshima and Nagasaki, hastening the end of World War II by killing nearly two hundred thousand people.

  Today: After decades of

international fear about the devastation that nuclear weapons can cause, no other nuclear bombs have been used during wartime.

- **1938:** Cancer is barely understood. The first cancer-causing agents, known as "carcinogens," have been isolated in England just five years before.

  Today: Cancer is the number two cause of death in the United States, but millions of dollars are spent on research each year, and much progress has been made in understanding causes and treatments.

- **1938:** The first steps in photocopy technology are made, as inventor Chester Carlson develops a method to reproduce an image on paper using electrostatic attraction.

  Today: Image reproduction has progressed to the point that computer users are transferring scanned images from one machine to another, without ever using paper to transmit them.

- **1938:** Orson Welles presents his radio program about an alien invasion, *War of the Worlds*, in the style of a news program. Across

America, hundreds of listeners believe that Martians are really invading Earth, and become panicked.

Today: Audiences are used to radio and television programs that use the same style as the news, and few people would take such a preposterous story seriously.

- **1938:** Radio and motion pictures are the main forms of entertainment in America. People living in urban areas attend live theater productions. Television technology is invented, but TV ownership is not widespread until after World War II.

  Today: Most homes own at least one television, many with the possibility of access to over five hundred channels at a time through cable and satellite systems.

- **1938:** Air travel is still an uncertain proposition. In 1937, aviator Amelia Earhart is lost at sea in the Pacific Ocean while trying to circumnavigate the globe. In 1938, Douglas Corrigan flies illegally from New York to Dublin, giving the excuse that his compass had led him in the wrong direction and earning him the nickname "Wrong-Way

Corrigan."

Today: International flights are routine, and all flight paths are monitored by the Federal Aviation Administration.

The Approach of World War II

Like America and many other countries around the world, Great Britain suffered through an economic depression in the 1930s. The country, which had started the century as the most powerful on Earth, was forced to take measures that would assure its continued economic stability. In 1931, for instance, the British government, which had been borrowing money from France and the United States to get by, imposed a heavy tariff on items that were brought into the country. This helped to control the economy, forcing British citizens either to buy goods that were made within the British Empire or to add tax money to the general revenue base. Although it helped the economic situation, British self-esteem suffered from this sign of economic weakness. The country's free trade policy had been a source of pride for Britain, and this forced abandonment of that policy was a clear sign that Great Britain no longer dominated the world the way it once had.

At the same time, Adolf Hitler and the Nazi party were rising to power in Germany. To a large extent, Hitler was able to gain power because of the same worldwide economic stagnation that was affecting America, Britain, and other countries. Germany was hit particularly hard, with prices of basic foods and supplies sometimes doubling within a week. Hitler was able to appeal to the suffering people, and he also addressed the matter of German pride, convincing the German people that the country was being mistreated by the international community. The Treaty of Versailles, which established the conditions for Germany's surrender in 1918, separated the states that had made up the German Republic, and placed restrictions on the country's armed forces, leaving Germany economically and militarily vulnerable. The Nazi party was voted into power in 1933 because the electorate believed that they could end the country's suffering and humiliation.

Almost immediately, Hitler's government began its program of military expansion. In the following years, German forces were used to absorb Yugoslavia, Czechoslovakia, and Poland, all of which it had given up to end the war. Looking back on it, many people wondered why the countries that had led the winning force in World War I did not stop Germany when it first started to violate the Treaty of Versailles. For one thing, many people across the world agreed with the German view that the treaty had been too confining and had caused the citizens of Germany to suffer more than they should have, and so there was not strong opposition to the steps Germany took to "correct" the situation. Another reason was that the economic crisis made countries in Western Europe, such as England and

France, reluctant to fight if they did not have to. Hitler signed new treaties with London, agreeing to limit the size of the German military, giving those who wanted to avoid war a chance to argue that it would be unnecessary. The forces opposing intervention into German affairs were so strong that the world ignored the stories that escaped from German territories of concentration camps where, it has been proven, millions of Jews, gypsies, and homosexuals were mutilated and killed.

Great Britain eventually did enter into war with Germany in 1939, after Hitler broke a nonaggression pact with Poland and attacked that country. By that time, it was clear that he intended to continue endless expansion and that treaties made no difference. At the start of the war, the brunt of opposing Hitler fell upon France, which was defeated by the Germans in 1940, and England, which was hammered by German bombing raids. Seventy thousand British civilians died during the war, which lasted until 1945.

Critical Overview

Rebecca is one of those novels that critics have a difficult time disrespecting. On the one hand, it does have excessive, overblown language in places, and its plot is far from original. On the other hand, the book's overwhelming approval by the general public, from its first printing in 1938 up through today, has made it in some respects immune to negative criticism, forcing reviewers to think twice before dismissing it as just one more popular romance. In general, critics have tended to take the time to find out what is effective in this novel and why it works, rather than just dismissing it because of its weaknesses.

Basil Davenport, reviewing *Rebecca* for the *Saturday Review* when it was first published, identifies the book as a mystery about who Rebecca really was and what happened to her, but he also credits du Maurier for writing so well and so compellingly that she does not have to rely on the murder mystery plot: "The book is skillfully contrived so that it does not depend only on knowledge of it for its thrill; it can afford to give no hint of it till two-thirds of the way through." Davenport goes on to explain that *Rebecca* is, after all, melodrama: the heroine, for one thing, is "at times quite incredibly stupid," such as when she takes advice from the housekeeper whom she knows hates her. He also points out "a forced heightening of the emotional values," a disreputable trick that melodrama relies on. Still, Davenport finds the novel "as absorbing a tale as the season is likely to bring."

As time went on, critics saw *Rebecca* outlive the usually short life cycle of popular romances, elbowing its way into a position in literary history. John Raymond, writing about it in the *New Statesman* in 1951, identifies du Maurier as "a poor woman's Charlotte Brontë" of the 1930s. He goes on to note, "Her *Rebecca*, whatever one's opinions of its ultimate merits, was a *tour de force*." He further suggests that du Maurier's fame may have made her a force for the literary world to reckon with but that her writing had become twisted by her commercial success so that she was then writing prose that was ready to be adapted to movies. Raymond's review of *My Cousin Rachel*, which came at the tail end of du Maurier's prolific period of one romantic bestseller after another, describes the book:

> … a honey for any Hollywood or Wardour Street tycoon. Slick, effective, utterly mechanical, the book is a triumphant and uncanny example of the way in which a piece of writing can be emasculated by unconsciously "having it arranged" for another medium.

Like Raymond, critics of the 1950s tended to cloud their judgments of du Maurier's writing with the tremendous financial success that it brought the author.

In the 1950s, du Maurier's style shifted as she focused on supernatural elements, particularly in her collection *Kiss Me Again, Stranger*. The short stories in that book were met with mixed enthusiasm. John Barkham's review in the *New York Review of Books* simply captures the acceptance of her style at the time by noting of the eight stories, "None of them is bad, and several are very good indeed." In particular, he points out the excellence of "The Birds," which was adapted years later to one of Alfred Hitchcock's most famous movies.

Throughout the 1950s and 1960s, du Maurier became better known as a writer of the supernatural, rather than as a romance writer who used supernatural elements to build suspense, as she had been after the success of *Rebecca*. Susan Hill, writing in 1971 about another collection of scary stories called *Not After Midnight*, notes that it was:

> … a good read, and most likely, a bestseller. If only the quality of the prose matched up to her inventiveness, if only the dialog were not so banal and the descriptions so flat, we might have something more than holiday reading on our hands.

With her popularity clearly established, and the reading public jumping at the chance to buy new novels from her, du Maurier moved, in later life, to writing about real-life subjects: her father, her grandfather, her early life, the countryside where she lived, and the occasional historical figure, such as Sir Francis Bacon. Critics tended to ignore her non-fiction works, or, if they did look them over, they approached them with a polite, patronizing attitude, suggesting that they viewed them as signs of a popular writer dabbling in a hobby. Of her book about Bacon, for instance, historian Pat Rogers notes, "Daphne du Maurier has many literary gifts, but I am not sure that this book has fully enlisted them." It is likely that a review of a book by a true historian would not have been so congenial and non-critical.

Sources

Barkham, John, Review in *New York Review of Books*, March 8, 1953, p. 8.

Davenport, Basil, "Sinister House," in *Saturday Review*, September 24, 1938, p. 5.

Hill, Susan, Review in *New Statesman*, July 23, 1971.

Raymond, John, Review in *New Statesman*, August 11, 1951.

Rogers, Pat, "Saving Her Bacon," in *Spectator*, Vol. 237, No. 7727, July 31, 1976, p. 20.

For Further Study

Auerbach, Nina, *Daphne du Maurier: Haunted Heiress*, University of Pennsylvania Press, 1999.

> This recent critical examination of du Maurier defends her against criticism that finds her work superficial.

Forster, Margaret, *Daphne du Maurier: The Secret Life of the Renowned Storyteller*, St. Martin's Press, 1994.

> This is the biography that was authorized by du Maurier's family. It has some probing information because the author had more access to papers and interviews than many du Maurier scholars.

Horner, Arvel, and Sue Zlisnik, *Daphne du Maurier: Writing, Identity and the Gothic Imagination*, St. Martin's Press, 1998.

> This relatively new study of the author's works concentrates on the supernatural elements with which she worked.

Vickers, Stanley, *The du Maurier Companion*, edited by Diana King, Fowey Rare Books, 1997.

> This reference work lists all of the novels, plays, films, and autobiographical works by du

Maurier and other literary members of her family.

Milton Keynes UK
Ingram Content Group UK Ltd.
UKHW021326270823
427564UK00021B/558